ALL OF US CAN FLY

After Motifs of Franz Kafka as Recounted by
STEFANIE GOLISCH

Musca Press
922 5TH ST
Ames, IA 50010
USA
www.muscapress.com
editor@muscapress.com
+1 (352) 388-3848
+1 (515) 462-0278

ALL OF US CAN FLY
© 2018 by Stefanie Golisch

All rights reserved. No part of this work covered by the copyright hereon may be reproduced or used in any form or by any means—graphic, electronic, or mechanical, including photocopying, recording, taping, or information storage and retrieval systems—without written permission of the publisher. The publisher makes no representation, express or implied, with regard of the accuracy of the information contained in this book and cannot accept any legal responsibility or liability for any errors or omissions that may be made.

ISBN-13:   978-1-941892-36-7

Cover: Modified drawing of Franz Kafka's *Mann zwischen Gittern*, 1924
Interior and cover design by polytekton.com

Acknowledgements

I am thankful to the *Franz-Edelmaier-Residenz für Literatur und Menschenrechte* (Merano) for the fellowship that inspired me to write this book. Also thanks to Andrew Goldthorp (Toronto) and Birgit Zybell (Milano) for their help with the English version of this book.

Life's splendor forever lies in wait around each one of us in all its fullness, but veiled from view, deep down, invisible, far off. It is there, though, not hostile, not reluctant, not deaf. If you summon it by the right word, by its right name, it will come.

From *Kafka's Journals*

Table of Contents

Acknowledgements   3

Description of a Struggle   9

A Crossbreed   13

Eleven Sons   17

Blumfeld, An Old Bachelor   19

Five Against One   23

The Bucket Rider   25

A Hunger Artist   29

A Report to an Academy   33

A Chinaman   39

A Message from the Emperor   43

In Front of The Law   45

The Winged   47

Description of a Struggle

Where is it written that you must be in a good mood
when you go to a party?
Maybe because of the other guests?
Because a party can be considered a success only
if you keep on laughing all the time?
This stupid party is covered with a sticky sugar glaze,
decorated with happy people,
the so called *good friends* of the host who, in truth,
cannot stand one another.

But I'm not in a good mood,
And do not have the least intention to be cheerful.
I hate pink lemonade and yellow
cream cake. I don't feel like clapping my hands,
when everybody else does.
I don't clap my hands but, instead,
spit out the cake in a high arc.

I stand up and move to a corner,
my arms crossed.
I'm the perfect spoil sport.

But they just won't leave me in silence.
There is one guest to whom no one pays attention.
Needing to confess himself, he tells me about a girl he has
kissed a few hours ago and with whom he has fallen in love.
And how can you not listen to someone who is in such a mood?
My ears open and close in the rhythm of his ramblings.

What on earth am *I* doing here?
What on earth is *he* doing here?
Come on, let's go for a walk, my friend.
Across this cold wintry night: One being in love,
the other being in the worst mood ever.
And while he talks about his girl,
I look up into the empty sky,
and I really don't know what to think of all this.

Then, suddenly, I fall flat
on the icy path.
While my companion keeps on talking
He's only interested in my ears being wide-open.

Just you wait, I'll show you alright!
I gather all my strength
and take a running jump on his back.

Now he has no choice:
He must obey me.
I spur my horse –
my friend, my *not* friend –
until he gets really wild.
I force him faster and faster up the mountain.

We fall just before
reaching the top of *mount Laurenzi*,
but not in the least do I dream of giving up.
And leave the unfortunate prey to a swarm of vultures
flying right towards us.

In the meantime, I, myself, have wings grown on my back.
And I'm just about to jump.

A Crossbreed

I have a very special pet,
it's a crossbreed between a cat and a lamb.
Out in the open air, he jumps around like a lamb,
at home, he stretches in the sun, just like a cat.

Nevertheless, he is afraid of cats and tries
to tear apart lambs.
There is no sound coming from his lips and
he fears the rats in the cellar.
I feed him with sweet milk
and if it were up to him,
he would spend all the time in the world
lying in my cozy bed.

We could live well together
if only there were no people around us!
Everybody wants to see my friend and at any cost.
With their own eyes.
They just won't let go and so, in the end, I accept:
Though only once a week!
And only for an hour!

I put on my Sunday clothes
and sit down by the window with my friend
on my lap.
I have tied a red ribbon around his neck.
We're ready!

And soon the first ones knock at our door.
With their two hundred questions
to which we, naturally, have no answer.
I just say: You have come to see him.
Here he is!
Look at him very carefully!

It happens that one of them
brings a cat or a lamb,
because they want to see his reaction.
They want to know finally to which race he
belongs, to the first or the second?

I say: you will never know,
but they just won't give up.
And when they at last leave,
I stroke my pet almost to death,
whispering in his ears sweet lies:
Don't worry, they won't come back.
Never ever.
We both know that this is not true,
but for a little while,
we feel a little better.

We understand each other
beyond words.
My pet is as faithful as a dog,
so many animals living in his wide, white soul.

But one day –
I had just taken a nap with him on my lap –
as I woke up I saw two tears
running down his face.
Or were they maybe my own?

Sometimes I get the feeling that
he wants to confide in me a secret.
His helplessness breaks my heart
and I pretend that I have already understood
his message.

He immediately calms down and begins
to dance for me and this looks really odd
and makes me feel even more
tender about him.
And how can you possibly think in those moments
oh, had he never been born or *if only he'd be already dead*?

Eleven Sons

I have eleven sons.
Eleven!
The fingers of both hands plus a thumb.
It would be easy to get confused, but I don't:
Because One
is ugly, but as wise as an old man.
Because Two
is good-looking and well-travelled.
Because Three
is also good-looking but inside him beats a heart of stone.
Because Four
is good-hearted and walks through life light-footed.
Because Five
is almost invisible. He is getting ready to become an important man.
Because Six
thinks a lot and talks even more.
Because Seven
laughs all the time but has no companion to laugh with.
Because Eight
is small and thin and the only one with a long beard.
Because Nine
is very smart and liked by women of all ages.
Because Ten
hasn't a single friend in the world.
Because Eleven
has a delicate health, but is strong inside and ready to fight.
These are my eleven sons and this is all I can say about them
today.
What I might say tomorrow, I cannot know today.
After all, where is it written that a father knows his sons?
And a son his father?

Blumfeld, An Old Bachelor

When Blumfeld, an old bachelor
comes home after a long day of work,
he is taken by a deep feeling of sadness
because he is all alone,
as lonely as a cloud.
No one awaiting him at home.
No one to ask him about his day.
No one who has prepared
a warm soup for him.

In those moments, Blumfeld,
a thin man with almost no hair left on his head,
gets tangled up in his thoughts.
He imagines himself in company of
a medium-sized dog,
a faithful friend that at night
would be there waiting for him behind
the entrance door,
counting impatiently his steps on the stairs.
He imagines how the dog welcomes him with joy,
wagging his tail and licking the fingers of his
master.
But how this dog stinks!
And how the whole house stinks of dog!

No, better not!
Better being alone than with
a dog that never cleans himself
and that leaves his hairs everywhere.
Every night, Blumfeld reaches the same conclusion.

Of course, there are also other types of pets,
canaries, gold fish,
turtles, probably as old as the world.
And all kind of plants.
And, yes, you can really get attached to
plants too, so they say.

Even if they have no eyes to look
into yours.
And that's maybe what a man needs most:
a pair of eyes, looking at you lovingly.

Blumfeld is sitting in his favorite armchair
and, still deep in thought,
he suddenly hears a strange noise.
A noise in this quiet house?
Where the hell does it come from?

It's not a dog barking,
nor a cat meowing.
Rather a certain click-clack which
comes from the next room.
Getting quite curious, Blumfeld gets up
to see what is happening.

There, behind the bedroom door,
two table-tennis balls are bouncing
up and down having, so it seems, great fun.

Come on, play with us, they shout,
but Blumfeld pretends not to have heard
their invitation. He is tired
and is not willing to play with them.
At his age!

Just you wait, my friends, now I get hold of you two,
he shouts in a menacing voice.
He starts running after the two little balls
which keep on bouncing more and more,
excited about their new,
quite unexpected play companion.

But still, Blumfeld has no intention to play.
He only wants to catch the balls.
But never will.
And even if, what would that change?

What could an old bachelor,
tired and sad, do with two
young and strong table-tennis balls?
And what could they do with him?

He stops in the middle of the room.
Bewildered.
What on earth was that all about?

Five Against One

We are five friends.
We all live in the same block.
During the day, we stand in front of the main gate
with crossed arms.
All in a row, one next to the other.
We won't let anyone through.
Everything is fine, except for the number six.
The one who wants to be with us,
but whom we do not want with us.
We want to be five not six.
There is nothing to understand about that,
and yet, he won't understand
that there is nothing to understand.
Every day he tries to join us and every day,
as soon as he turns up, we start to bark
unanimously.
But still, he just won't give up.
Every morning, he is there, staring at us.
But, alas, we want to be five and not six.

The Bucket Rider

Winter has come and
I haven't a piece of coal in my home.
Not a single lump.
What am I going to do now?
How am I going to cope?

I'm cold, says my stove, and I reply:
I'm cold, too.
What are we going to do now?
How are we going to cope?
I must go and get some coal,
but I haven't got a penny left.
What am I going to do now?
How am I going to cope?

There is no way:
I must go and get some coal, otherwise, this night,
I must die.
Without a penny in my pocket,
I mount the bucket of coal
and appoint it my horse.
Come on, let's go to the coalman,
you'll see, he won't send us home
empty handed.

No, I won't die this night,
and not even my stove will die.
No man and no stove will die.
We need just a little bit of coal.
Just enough for one night.
Tonight.

I knock, but there is no reply.
Behind the closed door I can hear
the coalman having an argument with his wife
He says yes. She says no.
Yes no yes no yes no.
No, we won't die tonight.

I beg you a bit of coal, please.
The cheapest one.
I swear, I will pay as soon as I can.
I beg you, please.

Yes no yes no yes no.
Finally, the door opens.
But it's not the coalman appearing,
it's his wife to chuck us away finally
with a cold shower.

I try again: I beg you.
Please.
But they pretend not to hear my pleading.

They don't want to hear.
They don't hear.

A Hunger Artist

People are no longer interested
in my very special art.
They don't understand anything.
They think that I'm exhibiting myself
because I like people looking at me,
because I love applauses,
because behind my art there is
something else hiding.

But my art has no secrets
I'm a hunger artist.
The thinnest of all.

I haven't been eating
since a lifetime.
I make them shut me in a cage and
a guardian checks that no food comes in.
That's all.
To see the spectacle of how much I can suffer,
people stand in a queue and buy a ticket.
They even bring their kids
to ask me a whole lot of questions.

Since when did I start doing this job?
If I never fancy any sweets?
If I don't feel lonely?
If I'm not afraid to die?
And this is what I reply:
I have been doing this job for all my life.
I never fancy any cakes or cookies.
I don't feel lonely.
And I'm not afraid of dying.

I say: I'm living in a cage with a little bit of straw
on the ground and I hardly ever sleep, because
the guardian is always keeping an eye on me.
This is my life.

I am a hunger artist.
I'm *the* hunger artist.

But people are less and less interested
in my very special art.
Everything has changed.
There was a time when I exhibited myself in big squares.
Now I'm living in a circus and
my cage is among those of the animals.

And, yet, I still love my art and I practice it
with even greater passion than before.
Since no one is looking at me any longer,
I have gone beyond my limits.

And soon I will have reached my final
goal:
I will disappear without leaving
any traces behind.

That's all I want to say.

My secret?
The secret, all children want to know?
Here it is:
I've become a hunger artist
because I have never found the food I really liked.
Had I found it, I would have eaten, just like you.

Like all of you…

A Report to an Academy

Honorable gentlemen of the Academy,
here I stand in front of you: a miracle
of science, living proof that
through the power of free will, an ape
can become a man!

Like you, honorable gentlemen, exactly like you.
Or almost.
Here is my story:
Once upon a time I was a free ape.
I was living in a big forest, jumping joyfully from
one tree to the next.
I didn't care about the next day.
I didn't care about anything.
Was I happy?
Maybe I was.
But to be honest, I don't remember or,
maybe, I simply didn't know
what happiness was.

I come from the Gold Coast.
One day, I was caught to be
transported to your cities:
For the delight of your children
And, also, to frighten your refined ladies.
It's easy to make fun of an ape
Anyone can do it.

But this is long time ago.
Nowadays, I don't make people laugh anymore.
And the proof is that you are no children and
that we are certainly not in a zoo,
but in a very important location.
In these venerable halls, laughter is not permitted.
Not even to me, no longer an ape,
but a man
Like you.
Or almost.

From the very beginning,
I was different from my companions.
I was ambitious,
I hated being in a cage,
I hated the bananas they threw at us,
since men believe that all apes love bananas.
But I was a very solemn ape.
And it was just a matter of time
that someone would have noticed my difference.
I was very certain about that.

Instead of accepting my fate,
I started to watch the world around me
carefully.
My guardians, for instance.
It was quite easy to imitate their gestures.
Far easier than I had expected.

First, I started to learn how to spit.
Secondly, how to hold a bottle of brandy
with both hands.
Thirdly, to drink the brandy
with the utmost ease.
People liked me.
I was clever, I learned fast.
In fact, I was becoming a man.

I had two options now:
Either the zoo or the circus
Without hesitating, I chose the circus,
certain that this would be the best place
to start a big career.
I would have become an attraction, a world celebrity,
the first ape man, dressed perfectly in a suit.
Smelling nicely and with impeccable manners,
a gentleman from head to toe.

With a white scarf round my neck
and a top hat on my head,
at night, I exhibited myself in front
of a sophisticated audience.
As the years went by I saw many cities
and got accustomed to many things.

Honorable gentlemen of the Academy,
today, by all rights, I can say that I am a man
of success.
It is true, I was born as an ape,
it is also true that I was caught to make children laugh,
but before the choice of remaining faithful to my nature
as an ape or becoming a traitor to improve my fate,
I chose the second.
I have become the most vicious enemy of myself.
Merciless, I chased the ape in me
to let the man be born out of it.

So please stand up, my dear gentlemen, and clap your hands.
Make me feel part of your wonderful human community
so that I can forget my unconditioned submission.
The huge shame of having betrayed my own beastly nature
and to have sold my soul for money and recognition.

Honorable gentlemen of the Academy,
applaud at the strictest ape hunter ever
who is talking to you at this very moment!
The only one who doesn't know only *one* but *two* deep truths:
The certitudes of science and culture and the certitudes
of the fleas and lice that
underneath my snow-white shirt can't wait for the moment
that I start to unbutton it...

A Chinaman

After an abundant meal,
I had just stretched out on the sofa
when my faithful servant, an excellent cook and
mother of my only child that died
a long time ago in his early years,
knocked on the door.
Someone had come to see me, she said,
a Chinaman.
A Chinaman? I replied quite astonished.
Dressed like they use to dress in China?
Yes, replied the old woman in a low submissive
servant's voice, it's exactly so.
Well then, ask this gentleman his name and
what he desires!
I've been living reclusively for my whole life,
so how could my name have travelled around the
entire world?
And yet, it seemed to be true. The Chinaman
wanted to see precisely me.
At this point I got up with great fatigue.
I'm a very tall man, very fat
and incredibly lazy.

Well then, let him in, I said rather annoyed,
while trying to adjust the collar of my shirt to
welcome my guest as a real gentleman.

Here you are, please, make yourself comfortable.
But as soon as the Chinaman saw me, he got pale
and jumped back.
It seemed, he was trying to escape.
But I was quicker and got hold of him in a delicate way,
pulling him by the belt of his long silky coat,
so that I could look at him at a close distance.
He was a short and thin man, most likely a
scholar, with a pair of big black glasses
and a small grey beard like that of a mountain goat.

To make him feel at ease, I bent down,
looking right into his deep black eyes and
lowering the voice as to confess to him a secret.
Please, I say, please take a seat and tell me about
your country, tell me about the world wandering
across the universe while I'm sleeping on my sofa
all the time…

A Message from the Emperor

The Emperor is dying.
What's that you say?
Dying? But the emperor is
immortal!
Don't be stupid. No human being is immortal.
And what about the message?
Well, his message is actually for you!
For me?
Yes. The emperor has whispered it into the ear of
the messenger and only after having it repeated
to him three times, did he leave.
But our country is huge and there are so many obstacles…
Well then? What is the message? What does it say?
And when will it arrive to me?
Don't be so impatient!
Just sit by the window and wait.
Wait.
And keep on waiting.

In Front of The Law

I was only a poor devil
that had left his village without any idea
where to go.
I didn't know anything about the world,
since I'd never been anywhere.
I didn't have a single penny in my pocket
and had no goal in mind.
I was tired of walking, I was cold and hungry
when I came to the front gate.
And asked the guardian to enter.
My whole story
is about me trying to enter the gate,
called the Law.
But I was just looking for a place to sleep,
so I kept on asking to enter, but the guardian
told me that it wasn't possible.
And would never be.
Time went by and I grew old and grey
without ever understanding the reason why.
I've been dead for quite some time now, and
I still don't know.
Why couldn't I enter that gate?
And why was it for me alone?

I simply cannot understand my story.

The Winged

Soon war will be over,
the enemy besieged. We're getting ready
to conquer the last city, singing at the top
of our voices. We're after screams and blood.
We will be the new heroes.
We advance road after road,
house after house, but there's no living soul around,
and how can we fill our great lust for
killing?
Finally, in the last house, an old man
approaches us, bent over double,
with two sad wings on his back.
Without saying a word, he stops
in front of our gang, looking straight
into our shameless eyes.
Why did you wait for us, I ask him,
why didn't you fly away, don't you have
two wings between your shoulder blades?
Don't you know why we came?
Impatient to kill, we wait for his answer.
Wings, he replies, are for flying and *not* flying.
I am old and tired, but if you want, I can tell you
a secret:
All of us can fly.
You too.

You too.

www.ingramcontent.com/pod-product-compliance
Lightning Source LLC
Chambersburg PA
CBHW022109040426
42451CB00007B/196